# Pursuing Purpose Mini Workbook

## 5 Keys to Fulfilling Your God-Given Purpose

### KYRA LANAE

GLORIOUS WORKS PUBLISHING
UPPER DARBY, PENNSYLVANIA

First Printing: 2019

ISBN: 978-1-7335565-3-8 (mini workbook)


ISBN: 978-1-7335565-1-4 (full workbook)

Glorious Works Publishing
201 Bywood Ave. #2214
Upper Darby, PA 19082
www.gloriousworkspublishing.com

Special discounts are available on bulk purchases or by corporations, associations, educators, and others. For details, contact publisher at admin@gloriousworkspublishing.com.

Glorious Works Publishing can bring authors to your live events. For more information or to book an event, contact Glorious Works Publishing at admin@gloriousworkspublishing.com or visit our website at www.gloriousworkspublishing.com.

## Dedication

To every woman who has wondered what, specifically, she was created for;

To every woman who has yearned for more meaning in her life;

To every woman who has wanted to experience true success and fulfillment;

To every woman who is pursuing purpose;

I dedicate this book to you.

## INTRODUCTION

Welcome to the Pursuing Purpose Mini Workbook: 5 Keys to Fulfilling Your God-Given Purpose. The Pursuing Purpose Mini Workbook is a mini version of the Pursuing Purpose Workbook, which is designed to propel women into discovering and fulfilling their purposes in every area of their lives. It will help you identify the purpose of your past, position, and passion among other key identifiers. You will answer questions such as: How can I apply what I have learned about my past to positively change my future? How does my reality compare with my expectations for the life stage that I am in right now? How can I become a solution to a problem that I'm passionate about? How much am I willing to pay of my time, energy and resources to achieve my goals and fulfill my purpose in life?

Pursuing Purpose will also give you practical next steps to take to assist you in seeing the manifestation of your goals, dreams and purpose. It is thought provoking and action inspiring. Whether you are a college student trying to figure out what your next steps are or you are well established in your life and career, but sense that there is more in life waiting for you, Pursuing Purpose is the bridge to help get you from where you are to where you need to be—living a purposeful life.

As you work through this mini workbook, take your time to digest, reflect and respond to the questions that are designed to probe your heart and mind. Provide, analyze and assess your responses. The more transparent and authentic that you are with yourself as you work your way through this workbook, the more beneficial it will be to you. Also, take advantage of my accompanying book, Pursuing Purpose: 5 Keys to Fulfilling Your God-Given Purpose. In the book, I share examples of my highs, lows, strengths and weaknesses, reflections and discoveries that projected me into living out my purpose. My experiences and responses are simply a guide for you. This mini workbook puts the focus on you and is designed to give you ample space to record and reflect on your responses and reinforce and elaborate on key concepts and ideas through worksheets, visuals, schedules, checklists and other resources. If you find this mini workbook to be helpful, take advantage of the full workbook with over 200 pages of information, reflections, and exercises.

Often, when we hear the idea of finding purpose in our lives, we think singularly, as if there is only one thing that we can or should do in life. The reality is that our purpose in life is to identify what we were created to do and do it in every area of our lives. This workbook will not only help you to pursue your purpose, but also uncover the hidden purposes in your life. As long as you are living, continue pursuing purpose.

<3 always,
Your sister in Christ,
Kyra Lanae

# KEY 1:

# DISCOVER PURPOSE IN YOUR

# PAST AND PAIN

past | noun

1. the time or a period of time before the moment of speaking or writing

pain | noun

1. physical suffering or discomfort caused by illness or injury or mental suffering or distress

# Key 1.1 What was my family life like growing up?

Did you grow up as an only child or were you in a long line of siblings? Were you raised by your parents, grandparents or maybe foster or adoptive parents? Did you have a close-knit extended family or did you grow up only knowing a few family members? What was the atmosphere like in your home? Was it warm, loving and comforting or was it cold and filled with despair?

As you walk down memory lane, deeply think about the mechanics and nuances of your family life. Discovering your past requires you to recall it and begin to dissect it. Subtle things that we overlooked growing up have significance in our lives. Both the unnoticed and profound details help shape who we are and how we perceive and function in our lives several years later.

Whatever the circumstances we found our family life, whether they were favorable or disheartening, they were significant and affected us into adulthood. Dissecting some of those circumstances can help decode the reasoning behind our choices and behaviors.

Now, you answer: What was my family life like growing up?

_____

_____

_____

_____

_____

_____

_____

_____

_____

_____

# The past

# is never

# where you think

# you left it.

Katherine Anne Porter

The role that faith played within my family was

_____
_____
_____

What I liked about my family was

_____
_____
_____

What I thought was strange about my family was

_____
_____
_____

What I wanted to replicate that I gleaned from my family was

_____
_____
_____

What I stayed away from that I witnessed or experienced within my family was

_____
_____
_____

Circle the character traits you possessed during your adolescent years. Underline the character traits that your closest group of friends possessed during your adolescent years. Place a check mark beside the character traits that the authority figures in your life possessed during your adolescent years.

| | | |
|---|---|---|
| Agreeable | Passionate | Unreliable |
| Authentic | Self-disciplined | Dishonest |
| Clean | Responsible | Greedy |
| Compassionate | Respectful | Discouraging |
| Cooperative | Trustworthy | Inconsiderate |
| Kind | Unselfish | Foolish |
| Optimistic | Brave | Obnoxious |
| Curious | Forgiving | Unhealthy |
| Educated | Aggressive | Prejudice |
| Ethical | Argumentative | Anxious |
| Grateful | Bossy | Impatient |
| Hardworking | Cowardly | Lazy |
| Innocent | Dangerous | Neglectful |
| Inventive | Devious | Fearful |
| Organized | Disobedient | Forgetful |
| Exciting | Petty | Envious |

I need to forgive_____

for_____

that happened_____.

I have been holding_____

captive for _____ days/weeks/months/years.

It is time to forgive_____.

I need to forgive_____

for_____

that happened_____.

I have been holding_____

captive for _____ days/weeks/months/years.

It is time to forgive_____.

I need to forgive_____

for_____

that happened_____.

I have been holding_____

captive for _____ days/weeks/months/years.

It is time to forgive_____.

## Color in the circles next to two characteristics from each group.

## Next, fill them in the blanks.

O Compassion

O Peace

O Confidence

O Other:_____

O Logic

O Honesty

O Desire to Help

O Other:_____

O Self- Discipline

O Love

O Commitment

O Other:_____

O Strength

O Lack of Self-Pity

O Forgiveness

O Other:_____

O Inner Drive

O Hope

O Courage

O Other:_____

O Faith

O Focus

O Resilience

O Other:_____

I possess

_____, _____,

_____, _____,

_____, _____,

_____, _____,

_____, _____,

_____ and _____,

to help me overcome my traumatic or painful experiences.

What do you feel each group listed is telling you about the direction in which you should take your life?

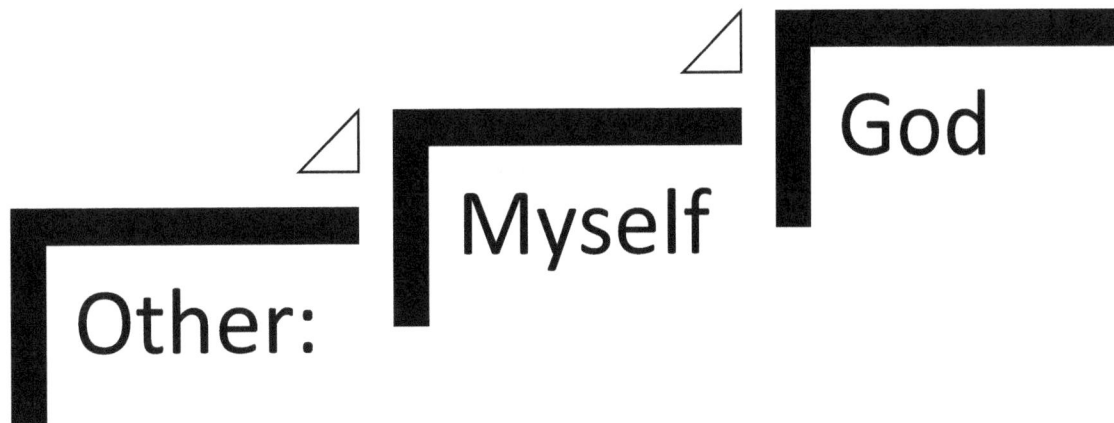

Society

Peers

Family

God

Myself

Other:

**Use the word bank to fill in the first blank in each group of words.**

**Next, complete the statements with your responses.**

**Word Bank:** Religions, Politics, History, Sexuality, Culture, Economics, Women's Rights, Racism, Parenting

When I encounter ideas that differ from my own as it relates to

I respond by

When I encounter ideas that differ from my own as it relates to

I respond by

When I encounter ideas that differ from my own as it relates to

I respond by

Circle the activities that you have done. Place a question mark next to the activities that you would be interested in doing. Place a check mark next to the activities that you enjoyed. Place an X next to the activities that you didn't enjoy.

Go to a concert

Go on a walk/run/hike

Pray

Cook a new recipe

Complete a DIY project

Go shopping

Stay in and watch a movie/favorite show

Clean your house

Go to a spa

Read a book

Go to the movies

Go to a nice restaurant

Paint

Go dancing

Start a blog

Get a manicure/pedicure

Travel

Rearrange your house/room

Complete brain teasers

Take a long, hot bath

Visit a museum

Go to the gym

Visit a library/bookstore

Browse photo albums

Read your Bible

Try a new workout class

Declutter/Organize

Find a new hobby

Go swimming

Complete a home improvement project

Sing karaoke

Bake a cake

Take a long drive

Explore nature

Turn off electronics

Volunteer

Hand write a letter to someone

Create a YouTube channel

Help a stranger

Take a free online class

Lay on a beach

Listen to a podcast

Get your finances in order

Make a time capsule

Learn to play a musical instrument

Write in your journal

Adopt a pet

11

## Time Tracker

**Label the topics that you frequently talk about. Start at the center of the circle. Move towards the outer ring, shading in to indicate how much time you spend talking about those topics. The more time you spend, the closer your shaded area will be to the outer ring.**

**What are the top three things that you spend the majority of your time talking about?** _____

How Much Time I Spend Talking About:

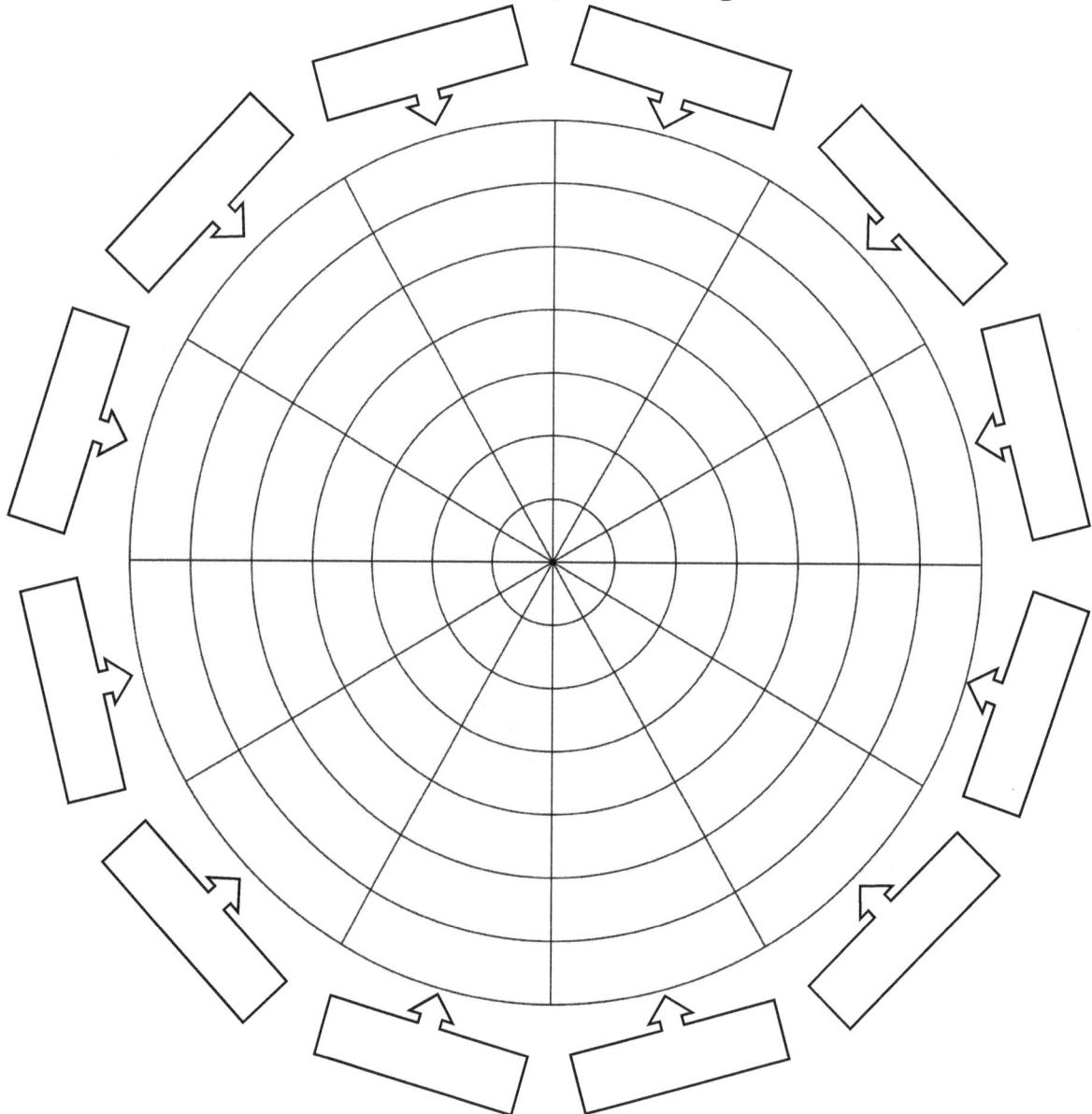

God has given each of you a gift from his great variety of spiritual gifts. Use them well to serve one another.

1 Peter 4:10-11

**Ask five people to identify your top ten strengths, talents and abilities.**

The ultimate test of man's conscience may be his willingness to sacrifice something today for future generations whose words of thanks will not be heard.

Gaylord Nelson

> **Use the graph to indicate what you expect your return on investments will be and periodically compare it to what your actual return on investments is over time.**

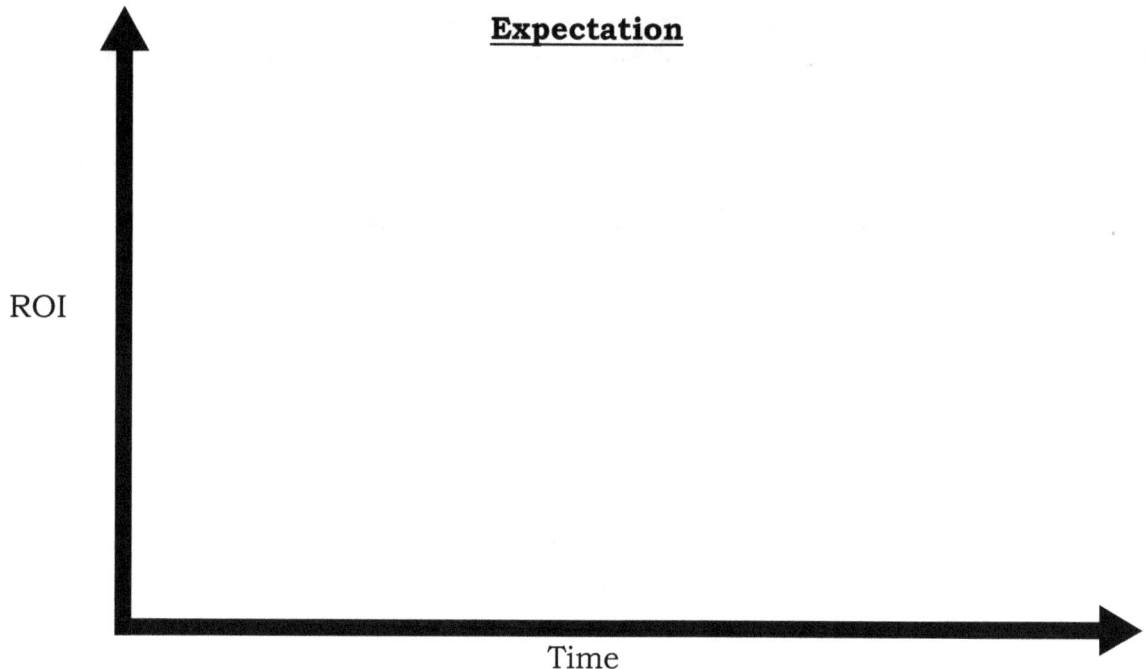

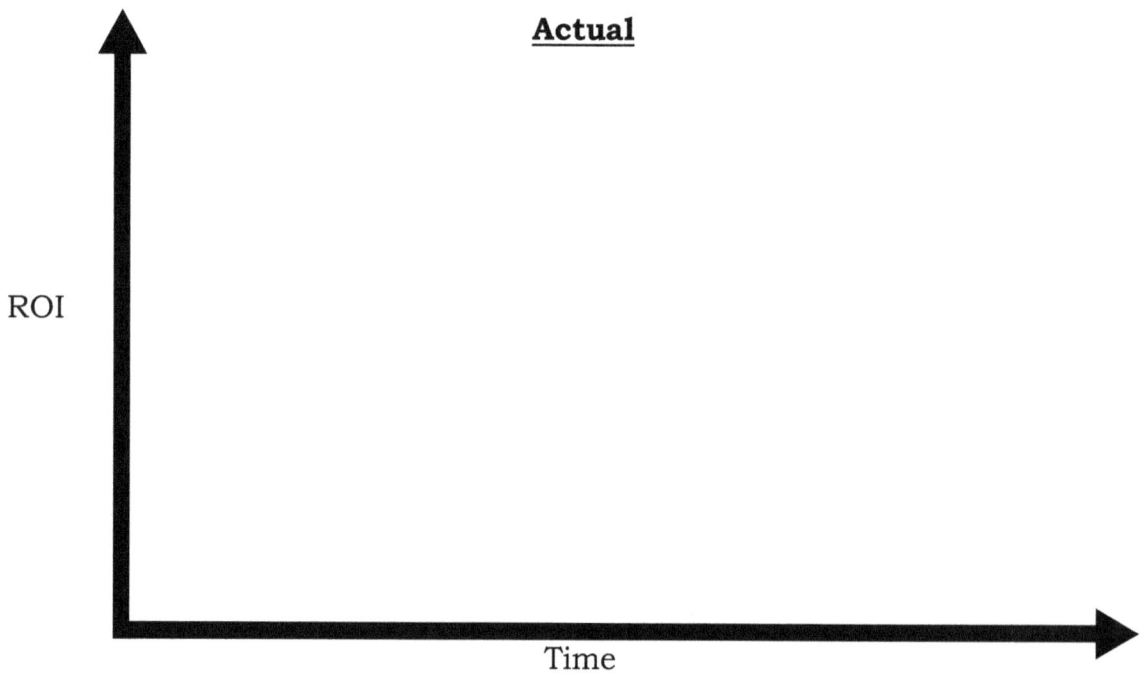

## <u>Expectation</u>

ROI

Time

## <u>Actual</u>

ROI

Time

16

**Mistake Tracker**

**Don't focus on the mistake. Focus on the time it takes you to identify, learn from and correct the mistake. The shorter the timespan, the better off you are.**

Mistake:

Lesson Learned:

Correction:

Time to Correct:

Mistake:

Lesson Learned:

Correction:

Time to Correct:

# Remember that failure is an event, not a person.

Zig Ziglar

## Set GREAT GOALS

**G**
- **GLORY**
- Does your goal bring **glory** to God?
- Is it ethical?

**R**
- **REACH**
- Does your goal **reach** other people?
- Does it benefit others?

**E**
- **EXPLICIT**
- Is your goal **explicitly** stated?
- Is it clear and detailed?

**A**
- **ASSESS**
- Is your goal able to be **assessed**?
- Can progress be evaluated?

**T**
- **TIMEFRAME**
- Does your goal have a **timeframe**?
- Does it have a deadline?

How can I apply what I have learned about my past to positively change my present and future? ( Reference Key 1.7)

Desired End Result:

_____

My Steps Systematically Working Backwards:

_____

_____

_____

_____

_____

How can I help prevent others from experiencing similar painful experiences as myself or help those who have already experienced similar painful experiences? (Reference Key 1.10)

Desired End Result:

_____

My Steps Systematically Working Backwards:

_____

_____

_____

_____

_____

## Think Space

This is your space to think, elaborate on a topic, if needed,

and write or draw.

**Make a note of the benefits you have received from sharing with others the purpose that you are pursuing.**

Motivation

Support

Accountability

Networking

Resources

Trusting God

For everything there is a season,

a time for every activity

under heaven...

A time to plant

and a time to harvest...

A time to tear down

and a time to build up...

A time to search

and a time to quit searching.

Ecclesiastes 3:1-6a

# Weekly Schedule Tracker

## What are your priorities?

### List them and use them to create your ideal schedule.

_____

_____

| | Ideal Schedule | Adjusted Schedule |
|---|---|---|
| **SUNDAY** | | |
| **MONDAY** | | |
| **TUESDAY** | | |
| **WEDNESDAY** | | |
| **THURSDAY** | | |
| **FRIDAY** | | |
| **SATURDAY** | | |

Some things work in theory but not in application. What worked in your initial schedule? Make adjustments, if needed.

_____

_____

**Habit Checker**

**It takes about 9 weeks for a habit to become automatic.**

**Keep track of your progress.**

Habit:

| | DAY 1 | DAY 2 | DAY 3 | DAY 4 | DAY 5 | DAY 6 | DAY 7 |
|---|---|---|---|---|---|---|---|
| WEEK 1 | | | | | | | |
| WEEK 2 | | | | | | | |
| WEEK 3 | | | | | | | |
| WEEK 4 | | | | | | | |
| WEEK 5 | | | | | | | |
| WEEK 6 | | | | | | | |
| WEEK 7 | | | | | | | |
| WEEK 8 | | | | | | | |
| WEEK 9 | | | | | | | |

## Distraction Tracker

### What are the things that are getting you off task from pursuing your purpose and achieving your goals?

Distraction                                          Frequency

|  | HOURLY | DAILY | 2-3X WEEK | WEEKLY | MONTHYLY | YEARLY |
|---|---|---|---|---|---|---|
|  |  |  |  |  |  |  |
|  |  |  |  |  |  |  |
|  |  |  |  |  |  |  |
|  |  |  |  |  |  |  |
|  |  |  |  |  |  |  |
|  |  |  |  |  |  |  |
|  |  |  |  |  |  |  |
|  |  |  |  |  |  |  |
|  |  |  |  |  |  |  |

# Key 5.6 Repeat

You did it! You accomplished that goal; you changed your career; you started your business; you wrote your book; you started your family; you led that ministry; you moved to that country; you received that degree. Now what? As you know, life goes on after you attain a goal or milestone. The beauty is that we were not created for a singular purpose, which once we discover and fulfill, that is it, we can now put our feet up and just glide aimlessly through the rest of our life. Wrong! That's not our original design.

Often when we hear people talk about discovering purpose or pursuing purpose, they say it as if it is only one thing. The truth is that we were created with purposes and our purposes are multifaceted. I believe there is an overarching purpose that we are all called to, which is to glorify God and to make disciples of Jesus Christ, but the way in which we carry out those purposes are unique to us. In every season and every situation, God has a purpose for us. When your car breaks down purely so that you can have a life-changing conversation with the mechanic, that is purpose being fulfilled. The key is to be able to recognize that purpose in every area of your life and maximize your opportunities to actively pursue it.

Throughout this book, you were able to discover purpose in your past, pain, position, posture, personality, passion, potential and payment. Each of those areas is essential. God can and wants to use every part of you—the good, the bad, the ugly and indifferent. As you continue to live out your purpose in life, periodically repeat these steps. Life's experiences and incremental knowledge have a way of changing our perspectives. What may have applied to you at one particular point in your life could drastically change at another point. As long as you are living, continue pursuing purpose.

## CONGRATULATIONS

_____

(Name)

# ON

# PURSUING YOUR PURPOSE

DATE: _____

SIGNED: KYRA LANAE

CONTINUE PURSUING PURPOSE UNTIL YOU FINISH THE RACE.

"I HAVE FOUGHT THE GOOD FIGHT,

I HAVE FINISHED THE RACE,

AND I HAVE REMAINED FAITHFUL."

2 TIMOTHY 4:7

# ABOUT THE AUTHOR

The question of *why* Kyra Lanae does what she does is more important than the question of *who* she is. Kyra Lanae's relationship with Jesus Christ and desire to please her Father, God, is the driving force behind everything she does. Whether writing books, speaking publicly, mentoring or encouraging others in her daily life, her heart's desire is to help people. As for *who* she is, Kyra Lanae is a Christ-follower and mother native to Philadelphia, Pennsylvania. Kyra Lanae currently resides in the Philadelphia Suburbs with her two wonderful children, Cameron Nasir and Sabrina Marie.

Kyra Lanae is an internationally known author, publisher, and dynamic, inspirational, and authentic speaker who empowers women worldwide in the areas of identity, purpose, relationships, parenting, ministry and writing. Kyra is the author of *Beauty for Ashes: The Transformation of my Life's Darkest Moments* and *Pursuing Purpose: 5 Keys to Fulfilling Your God-Given Purpose.* Kyra is also the founder and president of Glorious Works Publishing.

Kyra delivers wisdom and practical application as she shares her successes and failures transparently. Kyra is wise beyond her years which enables her to relate to women of all ages from Millennials to Baby Boomers. When she writes or speaks, you are sure to walk away with a new perspective, unearthed courage or reasonable next steps. She is like a gold miner of the heart, digging up precious treasures in the women whom she addresses. As women's identities, mindsets, and lives are transformed, so are their families, ministries, careers, businesses and communities. As Kyra pours strength into women, she motivates them to continue the cycle of strengthening other women. Women glean from the faith, hope and love that Kyra exudes as she walks women through her journey of overcoming rape, divorce, addictions and suicidal thoughts, just to name a few, and pursuing her God-given purpose in life.

Kyra Lanae has had the honor of being featured in *31Wife in Training*, an international Christian Women's magazine based out of Cape Town, South Africa. Kyra has also been a special guest and speaker for ministries and organizations including Gathering Connection Fellowship, Simplicity HealthStyle and CareerGPS. Kyra's refreshing spirit, wisdom, influence and contribution has opened the door for recurring invitations from every organization with whom she has partnered.

Kyra Lanae can be reached via email at admin@kyralanae.com or directly through her website, kyralanae.com. For booking, please visit kyralanae.com/booking. For publishing, please visit gloriousworkspublishing.com.

**More Titles by Kyra Lanae**

Beauty for Ashes: The Transformation of my Life's Darkest Moments

Pursuing Purpose: 5 Keys to Fulfilling Your God-Given Purpose

Pursuing Purpose Workbook: 5 Keys to Fulfilling Your God-Given Purpose

**Coming Soon by Kyra Lanae**

Oh, the Things That They Say: Life Lessons to Learn From the Silly Things That Kids Say

Moment by Moment Journal: Living Life After Losing a Loved One

Life Lessons for Kids Series: Will You Play With Me?

Purely Single: How to Successfully and Enjoyably Experience Purity and Singleness